ੴ ਸਤਿਗੁਰ ਪ੍ਰਸਾਦਿ

Business Entity Essentials

A quick guide to business structures and liability
protection in the USA

Dr. Satpreet Singh

Dedication

This book is dedicated to the Khalsa Panth, the embodiment of courage, righteousness, and selfless service. May this work be a tribute to the timeless values and teachings that inspire generations to live with integrity, compassion, and unwavering faith. Waheguru Ji Ka Khalsa, Waheguru Ji Ki Fateh.

Business Entity Essentials: A Quick Guide to Business
Structures and Liability Protection in the USA

LCCN: 2024945756

ISBN: 978-1-963353-00-6   (Print)
ISBN: 978-1-963353-01-3   (Electronic)

Printed in the USA by Sikh Reference Library USA
(www.sikhreferencelibraryusa.org)

Disclaimer

This book provides very basic information to help readers understand the different types of business entities and liability protection. It is written to give a general overview of various business structures, helping individuals and entrepreneurs decide which option might best suit their business and personal needs. For more detailed and tailored advice, it is highly recommended to consult with a tax professional, attorney, or accountant to ensure the right business type is chosen for specific circumstances. This book serves as an informational guide only and does not provide professional legal or financial advice.

Contents

*****

Sole Proprietor

A sole proprietorship is the simplest and most common type of business structure. It means that one person owns and runs the business. The owner and the business are legally considered the same, so the owner is personally responsible for any debts, losses, or legal actions the business might face. There's no need to file formal paperwork to create a sole proprietorship, making it an easy and affordable option to start a business.

In this structure, the business income is reported on the owner's personal tax return, which simplifies taxes. However, because there's no legal separation between personal and business assets, the owner's personal property (like a home or car) can be at risk if the business faces financial trouble. Sole proprietorships are ideal for small businesses or individual entrepreneurs who want to start quickly with a minimal setup.

There are two main types of sole proprietorships: **Independent Sole Proprietorship** and **Franchise Sole Proprietorship**. In an Independent Sole

Proprietorship, the owner runs a business they created on their own, such as a freelance service, retail shop, or consulting firm. The owner has full control over operations and decision-making. In a Franchise Sole Proprietorship, the owner operates under a larger company's brand and business model, such as running a franchise of a well-known restaurant or retail chain. While the franchisee owns the business, they must follow the established guidelines set by the franchisor. Both types provide the benefits of simplicity and control but come with the same personal liability risks.

Sole-Proprietor Formation Type

Same as the owner's name

- **Definition:** A business owned and operated by a single individual with no legal distinction between the owner and the business.

- **Ownership:** One person is responsible for the business.

- **Legal Liability:** The owner is personally liable for all business debts and obligations.

There is no separation between personal and business assets.

- **Taxes:** The income from the business is reported on the owner's personal tax return (Schedule C on Form 1040 in the U.S.).

- **Registration:** No need to file formation documents with the state, but local business licenses may be required.

Doing Business As (DBA)

- **Definition:** A DBA is a way to register a business name other than the business owner's legal name (in a sole proprietorship) or the legal name of an entity (like an LLC or corporation).

- **Purpose:** It allows sole proprietors or entities to operate under a name other than their own legal name.

- **Legal Impact:** A DBA does not provide legal protection or a separate legal identity. It's simply a naming tool.

- **Registration:** The DBA must be registered with the state or local government (depending on the region).

Fictitious Business Name (FBN)

- **Definition:** An FBN is essentially the same as a DBA. The term is used interchangeably in many regions.

- **Purpose:** It allows individuals or entities to legally operate under a name other than their personal name or the name of their registered business.

- **Legal Impact:** Like a DBA, it doesn't create a separate legal entity or provide legal protections.

- **Registration:** Need to file a FBN statement with the county or state government, depending on local laws.

Key Differences

- **Sole Proprietorship** is a business structure where an individual owns and runs the business, with no legal separation between the owner and the business.

- DBA and FBN are naming conventions, not business structures. They allow a business, whether it's a sole proprietorship, LLC, or corporation, to operate under a different name from the owner's or the entity's legal name.

- DBA and FBN don't provide any liability protection or change the business's legal structure. They are just ways to register a business under an alternative name for branding or legal purposes, while Sole Proprietorship defines the entire business framework.

*****

Partnership

A **partnership** is a business structure where two or more individuals share ownership and work together to run the business. Each partner contributes to the business, whether through money, property, skills, or labor, and in return, they share the profits, losses, and decision-making responsibilities. Partnerships offer flexibility in how they are managed, allowing the partners to decide how tasks are divided and how the business will operate.

One of the advantages of a partnership is that it is relatively easy to form, requiring fewer formalities than corporations or LLCs. However, partnerships come with shared legal and financial responsibilities. This means that each partner is personally liable for the business's debts and obligations, and the actions of one partner can impact all partners. Despite the potential risks, partnerships can be a great option for people who want to combine resources and expertise to build a business together.

Types of Partnerships

General Partnership (GP)

- **Definition:** A business structure where two or more individuals share ownership, profits, losses, and management responsibilities.

- **Legal Liability:** All partners share unlimited personal liability for the debts and obligations of the business.

- **Management:** Each partner has equal rights to manage the business unless otherwise agreed upon.

- **Taxes:** General partnerships are subject to **pass-through taxation**. The partnership itself files an **IRS Form 1065 (U.S. Return** of Partnership Income), which reports the partnership's income, deductions, and credits. The profits and losses are then passed through to the partners, who report them on their personal tax returns.

Limited Partnership (LP)

- **Definition:** A partnership with at least one general partner and one or more limited partners.

- **General Partner:** Manages the business and is personally liable for its debts.

- **Limited Partner:** Invests in the business but has limited liability and cannot participate in management.

- **Taxes:** Like general partnerships, limited partnerships file an **IRS Form 1065**, and income is passed through to both general and limited partners, who report it on their personal tax returns.

Limited Liability Partnership (LLP)

- **Definition:** A partnership where all partners have limited liability protection from the actions of the other partners.

- **Legal Liability:** Partners are not personally liable for the debts of the partnership or for the actions of other partners.

- **Management:** Each partner can manage the business.

- **Taxes:** LLPs also file an **IRS Form 1065**, and the profits and losses pass through to the individual partners' personal tax returns, similar to general partnerships.

Joint Venture (JV)

- **Definition:** A temporary partnership between two or more entities or individuals for a specific project or venture.

- **Duration:** Typically created for a specific project or limited time.

- **Legal Liability:** Liability depends on the terms of the joint venture agreement.

- **Taxes:** Generally treated as a partnership for tax purposes, requiring the filing of **IRS Form 1065**, with income being passed through to the joint venture partners.

Silent Partnership

- **Definition:** A partnership where one or more "silent" partners contribute capital but do not actively participate in management.

- **Legal Liability:** Silent partners typically have limited liability, meaning they are not personally responsible for the partnership's debts beyond their investment, depending on the partnership agreement. The general partners, if any, are responsible for managing the business and have unlimited liability.

- **Management:** The business management is handled entirely by the active or general partners. Silent partners have no involvement in the day-to-day operations or decision-making processes, as their role is solely as financial backers.

- **Taxes:** Like other partnerships, the partnership must file an **IRS Form 1065 (U.S. Return of Partnership Income)** to report its income, deductions, and credits. Income from the partnership is passed through to the silent partners, who report it on their personal tax returns.

Partnership Limited by Shares

- **Definition:** A hybrid form of partnership where capital is divided into shares, and partners' liability is limited to their shareholding.

- **Legal Liability:** Partners' liability is limited to the amount they have invested in the business through shares.

- **Management:** Generally, the management is handled by one or more general partners, while others are shareholders.

- **Taxes:** Pass-through taxation applies, and the partnership files **IRS Form 1065**.

Master Limited Partnership (MLP)

- **Definition:** A publicly traded partnership that operates in certain industries, such as energy or natural resources.

- **Ownership:** Limited partners own shares that are traded on a public exchange, while a general partner manages the day-to-day operations.

- **Legal Liability:** Limited partners have liability protection, while the general partner has full liability.

- **Management:** Managed by a general partner, who typically holds operational control.

- **Taxes:** MLPs enjoy pass-through taxation, avoiding corporate taxes, but unit holders (limited partners) pay taxes on distributions.

- **Purpose:** Popular in industries like oil, gas, and energy infrastructure, allowing public investors to invest in partnerships.

Unincorporated Association

- **Definition:** A group of individuals who come together for a common purpose but without forming a formal legal entity.

- **Ownership:** No formal ownership; members share responsibility and decision-making.

- **Legal Liability:** Since the association is not a separate legal entity, members can be personally liable for its debts or obligations.

- **Management:** Typically managed informally by the members.

- **Taxes:** No formal tax status; income generated by the association may be taxable to individual members.

- **Purpose:** Often used by non-profit organizations, clubs, or community groups that do not wish to incorporate formally.

Syndicate

- **Definition:** A temporary alliance of individuals or entities formed to manage and finance a specific project or venture, often in real estate or investments.

- **Ownership:** Each member invests capital and owns a portion of the syndicate.

- **Legal Liability:** Liability depends on the specific structure chosen (e.g., partnership or LLC).

- **Management:** Typically managed by a lead member or managing entity.

- **Taxes:** Taxation depends on the underlying structure chosen for the syndicate (e.g., partnership, LLC, or corporation).

- **Purpose:** Commonly used for real estate investments, joint ventures, or funding large projects.

*****

Limited Liability Company (LLC)

A **Limited Liability Company (LLC)** is a business structure that combines the some or most benefits of both corporations and partnerships. It provides **limited liability protection** to its owners (called members), meaning the members' personal assets (such as their home or personal savings) are protected from business debts and liabilities.

An LLC offers flexibility in **management** and **taxation**. It can be managed by its members (member-managed) or by appointed managers (manager-managed). In terms of taxation, an LLC can be taxed as a **sole proprietorship** (for single-member LLCs), a **partnership** (for multi-member LLCs), or it can elect to be taxed as a **corporation** (either S-Corp or C-Corp).

LLCs are popular because they provide liability protection without the complexity and formalities that corporations often require, making them a flexible and straightforward option for small businesses and entrepreneurs.

Single-Member LLC

- **Definition:** An LLC with only one owner (member).

- **Legal Liability:** Provides limited liability protection to the single member, meaning their personal assets are protected from business debts and obligations.

- **Management:** Managed by the single owner, but they can also appoint a manager.

- **Taxes:** By default, taxed as a sole proprietorship (disregarded entity) for tax purposes, but the owner can elect to be taxed as a corporation (S-Corp or C-Corp).

Multi-Member LLC

- **Definition:** An LLC with two or more owners (members).

- **Legal Liability:** Provides limited liability protection to all members, separating personal assets from business liabilities.

- **Management:** Can be either **member-managed** (where members run the business) or **manager-managed** (where members appoint one or more managers to run the business).

- **Taxes:** By default, taxed as a partnership, with profits and losses passed through to members. Members can also elect to be taxed as a corporation (S-Corp or C-Corp).

Member-Managed LLC

- **Definition:** An LLC where all members participate in the day-to-day management and decision-making.

- **Management:** The members are responsible for the running of the business and making key decisions.

- **Legal Liability:** Members have limited liability protection.

- **Taxes:** Can be taxed as a sole proprietorship (single-member), partnership (multi-member), or elect to be taxed as a corporation (S-Corp or C-Corp).

Manager-Managed LLC

- **Definition:** An LLC where the members appoint one or more managers to run the day-to-day operations.

- **Management:** Managers (who can be members or non-members) are responsible for managing the business, while members take on a more passive role.

- **Legal Liability:** Members retain limited liability protection.

- **Taxes:** Can be taxed as a sole proprietorship, partnership, or elect for corporate taxation.

Series LLC

- **Definition:** A unique form of LLC that allows for the creation of separate "series" or divisions within the LLC. Each series operates independently and can have its own assets, liabilities, and members.

- **Legal Liability:** Each series within the LLC has its own liability protection, so if one series is sued, the other series are not affected.

- **Management:** Each series can have its own management structure.

- **Taxes:** The IRS generally treats each series as a separate entity for tax purposes, though tax treatment may vary by state.

Professional LLC (PLLC)

- **Definition:** An LLC formed by licensed professionals (e.g., doctors, lawyers, accountants) who are legally required to form a special type of LLC due to professional licensing regulations.

- **Legal Liability:** PLLCs provide limited liability protection for business debts and obligations, but members are typically personally liable for their own professional malpractice or negligence.

- **Management:** Can be member-managed or manager-managed.

- **Taxes:** Taxed the same as a regular LLC, with options for sole proprietorship, partnership, or corporate tax treatment.

Low-Profit LLC (L3C)

- **Definition:** A hybrid between a nonprofit organization and an LLC, designed to pursue socially beneficial, charitable goals while allowing for profit-making.

- **Legal Liability:** Offers limited liability protection for its members.

- **Management:** Managed by members or managers, depending on the structure.

- **Taxes:** Taxed as a regular LLC, but the L3C's primary purpose must be to serve a charitable or educational cause rather than generate profits.

Foreign LLC

- **Definition:** An LLC that operates in a state other than the one where it was originally formed. The LLC must register as a "foreign LLC" in the new state where it intends to conduct business.

- **Legal Liability:** Offers the same limited liability protection as a domestic LLC.

- **Management:** Managed according to the original LLC agreement (can be member-managed or manager-managed).

- **Taxes:** Subject to state taxes in the new state where it operates, in addition to the original state.

Anonymous LLC

- **Definition:** An LLC designed to protect the privacy of its owners by not requiring the disclosure of member identities in public records.

- **Legal Liability:** Provides limited liability protection while keeping ownership information private.

- **Management:** Managed in the same way as other LLCs (member-managed or manager-managed).

- **Taxes:** Taxed as a regular LLC (sole proprietorship, partnership, or corporate tax election).

Converting an LLC to an S-Corporation (S-Corp) Taxation

The LLC must meet the following eligibility requirements for S-Corp taxation status.

- Be a domestic business.

- Have no more than 100 shareholders (members).

- All shareholders must be U.S. citizens or residents.

- All shareholders must be individuals (not corporations or partnerships).

- Have only one class of stock.

File Form 2553 (Election by a Small Business Corporation).

- **Deadline:** To elect S-Corp taxation for the current tax year, Form 2553 must be filed within two months and 15 days of the start of the tax year.

- **IRS Approval:** After filing, the IRS sends confirmation of the S-Corp election.

Operational and Accounting Changes (Optional)

- **Payroll Requirements:** S-Corps must pay reasonable salaries to members who work for the business, and payroll taxes must be withheld.

- **Distributions:** After paying a reasonable salary, the remaining profits distribution as dividends are not subject to self-employment taxes.

Benefits of S-Corp Taxation for LLC

- **Avoidance of Double Taxation:** Only the shareholders (members) are taxed on the company's income.

- **Reduction in Self-Employment Taxes:** Members only pay self-employment tax on their salary, not on the distributions.

Converting an LLC to a C-Corporation (C-Corp) Taxation

File IRS Form 8832 (Entity Classification Election)

- **Purpose:** To elect for the LLC to be taxed as a corporation.

- **Election Type:** Check the box to elect taxation as a **C-Corporation**.

- **Deadline:** The form must be filed within 75 days of the start of the tax year for the election to be retroactive to the beginning of that year.

Operational and Accounting Changes (Optional)

- **Separate Taxation:** C-Corp itself pays corporate taxes (currently at a flat federal rate), and then shareholders pay taxes on dividends they receive (double taxation).

- **Corporate Formalities:** Although the LLC doesn't legally change to a C-Corp, maintaining corporate records, issuing stock, and holding shareholder meetings are recommended for C-Corp tax election.

Benefits of C-Corp Taxation for LLC

- **Potential Tax Deferral:** Profits can be retained in the business, taxed at the corporate rate, and not distributed as dividends.

- **Access to Corporate Tax Deductions and Credits:** C-Corps may benefit from certain tax credits and deductions not available to LLCs or S-Corps.

Important Considerations for Both S-Corp and C-Corp Elections

- **Legal Structure Remains LLC:** The LLC remains legally an LLC, but it will be treated as a corporation for tax purposes.

- **State-Level Considerations:** Some states may have additional filing requirements or different treatment of LLCs electing S-Corp or C-Corp status.

- **Payroll Requirements:** For both S-Corp and C-Corp, if members work for the business, they must be treated as employees and receive a reasonable salary.

*****

Corporation

A **corporation** is a legal business entity separate from its owners, called shareholders. This separation provides **limited liability protection**, meaning shareholders are not personally responsible for the corporation's debts or legal obligations. Their liability is limited to the amount they have invested in the corporation. Corporations are managed by a **board of directors** that makes key decisions, while **officers** (such as a CEO or CFO) handle day-to-day operations. Corporations can raise capital by issuing stock shares, making them attractive for larger businesses seeking investment.

Corporations are subject to specific legal requirements, including filing **Articles of Incorporation** and following corporate governance rules. They also face **double taxation** in the case of C-Corporations: the corporation pays taxes on its profits, and shareholders pay taxes on dividends they receive. However, S-Corporations can avoid double taxation by passing income directly to shareholders, who report it on their personal tax returns. Corporations offer a solid structure for growth and investor opportunities but have more regulatory and administrative requirements than other business structures like LLCs or partnerships.

C-Corporation (C-Corp)

- **Definition:** A standard corporation that is taxed separately from its owners.

- **Ownership:** Unlimited number of shareholders; ownership is represented by stock shares.

- **Legal Liability:** Provides limited liability protection to shareholders—personal assets are generally protected from the company's liabilities.

- **Management:** Managed by a board of directors, who oversee corporate decisions, while day-to-day operations are handled by officers.

- **Taxes:** Subject to **double taxation**: the corporation pays taxes on its income (corporate tax rate), and shareholders pay taxes on dividends received.

- **Benefits:** There are no restrictions on the number of shareholders or their nationality, and the company is flexible in issuing different classes of stock.

S-Corporation (S-Corp)

- **Definition:** A special type of corporation that allows pass-through taxation, similar to an LLC or partnership.

- **Ownership:** Limited to 100 shareholders, and all must be U.S. citizens or residents. Only individuals can be shareholders, not other corporations or partnerships.

- **Legal Liability:** Shareholders enjoy limited liability protection.

- **Management:** Similar to C-Corps, with a board of directors and officers managing the company.

- **Taxes:** S-Corps avoid double taxation. The corporation's income is passed through to shareholders, who report it on their personal tax returns.

- **Benefits:** Pass-through taxation helps avoid double taxation; still enjoys the limited liability of a corporation.

- **Restrictions:** Must meet specific IRS criteria to qualify, including the one class of stock rule and shareholder restrictions.

Professional Corporation (PC)

- **Definition:** A corporation formed by licensed professionals (e.g., doctors, lawyers, architects, etc.) who offer professional services.

- **Ownership:** Only licensed professionals in the same field can be shareholders.

- **Legal Liability:** Provides limited liability protection for business debts, but shareholders may be personally liable for professional malpractice.

- **Management:** Managed similarly to other corporations with a board of directors and officers.

- **Taxes:** Can be taxed as a C-Corp or S-Corp, depending on the election made.

- **Benefits:** Offers limited liability and is specifically tailored for professional services businesses that require personal licensure.

Close Corporation (Closed-Corp)

- **Definition:** A corporation with a small number of shareholders that does not publicly trade shares.

- **Ownership:** Limited number of shareholders, typically family members or close associates.

- **Legal Liability:** Offers limited liability protection for shareholders.

- **Management:** Often more informal than a traditional corporation. Shareholders may have more direct control over business decisions and bypass the typical board of directors structure.

- **Taxes:** Can be taxed as either a C-Corp or S-Corp, depending on the corporation's election.

- **Benefits:** Simplified corporate structure with more flexibility in management and less regulatory scrutiny compared to a publicly traded corporation.

- **Restrictions:** Not allowed to publicly sell shares, and usually, there are limits on the number of shareholders.

Nonprofit Corporation (501(c)(3))

- **Definition:** A corporation organized for charitable, educational, religious, literary, or scientific purposes. These corporations are exempt from paying federal income taxes if they meet IRS requirements.

- **Ownership:** There are no shareholders; instead, a board of directors governs the corporation. Surplus revenue must be reinvested into the organization's mission.

- **Legal Liability:** Directors and officers are generally shielded from personal liability for the organization's debts and liabilities.

- **Management:** Managed by a board of directors, with officers running daily operations.

- **Taxes:** Exempt from federal and some state taxes if they qualify under IRS section

501(c)(3). Donations made to the organization may also be tax-deductible for donors.

- **Benefits:** Tax-exempt status; can receive tax-deductible donations.

- **Restrictions:** Profits cannot be distributed to members or directors; they must follow strict IRS guidelines regarding purpose and operation.

Benefit Corporation (B-Corp)

- **Definition:** A for-profit corporation that commits to creating a public benefit and generating profit.

- **Ownership:** Similar to C-Corps, with shareholders who own stock in the company.

- **Legal Liability:** Provides limited liability protection to shareholders.

- **Management:** Managed by a board of directors, with the additional responsibility of considering the impact of decisions not just on shareholders but on society, workers, and the environment.

- **Taxes:** Taxed as a regular for-profit corporation (usually as a C-Corp), subject to both corporate and shareholder taxes.

- **Benefits:** Ability to balance profit and mission; built-in legal protections for mission-driven businesses.

- **Restrictions:** Required to publish an annual benefit report showing progress in achieving social and environmental goals.

Public Corporation

- **Definition:** A corporation whose shares are publicly traded on stock exchanges (e.g., NYSE or NASDAQ).

- **Ownership:** Owned by the general public through shares of stock, and ownership can be widely dispersed.

- **Legal Liability:** Shareholders have limited liability protection.

- **Management:** Managed by a board of directors, and subject to greater regulatory oversight (e.g., SEC filings, Sarbanes-Oxley compliance).

- **Taxes:** Subject to corporate taxes, and shareholders are taxed on dividends received, resulting in double taxation.

- **Benefits:** Access to capital through public markets; potential for rapid growth.

- **Restrictions:** Must comply with extensive regulatory requirements and reporting.

Cooperative Corporation (Co-op)

- **Definition:** A corporation owned and operated by its members for their mutual benefit.

- **Ownership:** Owned by members who use the cooperative's services; each member typically has an equal vote.

- **Legal Liability:** Provides limited liability protection to its members.

- **Management:** Managed democratically by its members, with decisions often made on a one-member, one-vote basis.

- **Taxes:** Co-ops can distribute profits (called patronage dividends) to members, which may be tax-deductible.

- **Benefits:** Democratic control by members, profits are shared with members rather than external shareholders.

- **Restrictions:** Must operate for the benefit of its members, not external shareholders.

Joint-Stock Corporation

- **Definition:** A corporation with ownership divided into transferable shares of stock.

- **Ownership:** Shareholders own stock, which can be freely traded (similar to a public corporation).

- **Legal Liability:** Shareholders have limited liability protection.

- **Management:** Managed by a board of directors, similar to other corporations.

- **Taxes:** Subject to corporate taxation and double taxation on dividends.

- **Benefits:** Allows for the free transferability of shares, providing flexibility for investors.

*****

Trust

A **trust** is a legal arrangement in which one party, known as the **trustor** (or settlor), transfers assets to another party, called the **trustee**, to manage for the benefit of a third party, known as the **beneficiary**. The trustee holds and manages the assets according to the terms outlined in the trust agreement.

Trusts are commonly used in estate planning to ensure that assets are distributed to beneficiaries in a specific manner. There are different types of trusts, including **revocable trusts**, which can be altered or revoked by the trustor during their lifetime, and **irrevocable trusts**, which cannot be changed once established.

One of the main benefits of a trust is that it can help bypass probate, ensuring a more efficient transfer of assets upon death, and it can also provide protection from creditors or estate taxes in certain cases. Trusts are also used to manage assets for individuals who may not be able to handle them on their own, such as minors or people with special needs.

Living Trust (Inter Vivos Trust)

- **Definition:** A trust created during the grantor's lifetime to manage their assets.

- **Revocable or Irrevocable:** Can be **revocable** (the grantor can modify or revoke it during their lifetime) or **irrevocable** (cannot be changed or revoked after it's established).

- **Purpose:** Primarily used for estate planning, allowing assets to bypass probate upon death.

- **Trustee:** Typically, the grantor serves as the trustee during their lifetime, with a successor trustee taking over upon death or incapacitation.

- **Benefits:** Avoids probate, provides privacy, and allows seamless management of assets during the grantor's life and after death.

Revocable Trust

- **Definition:** A type of living trust where the grantor retains the ability to alter, amend, or revoke the trust at any time during their lifetime.

- **Purpose:** Typically used for estate planning, to avoid probate and maintain control over assets.

- **Trustee:** The grantor often serves as the trustee, with a successor trustee named to manage assets after the grantor's death.

- **Benefits:** The flexibility to change terms or revoke the trust avoids probate and provides continuity of asset management.

- **Drawbacks:** Does not offer asset protection from creditors during the grantor's lifetime.

Irrevocable Trust

- **Definition:** A trust that, once established, cannot be altered, amended, or revoked by the grantor without the beneficiaries' consent.

- **Purpose:** Used for estate tax reduction, asset protection, and charitable giving.

- **Trustee:** The grantor appoints a trustee, but the grantor cannot usually serve as trustee.

- **Benefits:** Protects assets from creditors and lawsuits and may reduce estate taxes.

- **Drawbacks:** Loss of control over assets once transferred to the trust.

Testamentary Trust

- **Definition:** A trust that is created upon the death of the grantor, as specified in their will.

- **Revocable or Irrevocable:** It becomes **irrevocable** after the grantor's death.

- **Purpose:** Provides for the management and distribution of the grantor's assets after death.

- **Trustee:** The trustee is named in the will and is responsible for managing the assets.

- **Benefits:** Can provide for minor children, manage assets, or distribute wealth according to specific terms after death.

- **Drawbacks:** Subject to probate since it is created by the will.

Asset Protection Trust

- **Definition:** A trust designed to protect the grantor's assets from creditors, lawsuits, and claims.

- **Revocable or Irrevocable:** Usually **irrevocable**, but some jurisdictions allow **self-settled** asset protection trusts that offer some control.

- **Purpose:** Shields assets from creditors and legal judgments.

- **Trustee:** A third-party trustee often manages the trust.

- **Benefits:** Provides a high level of asset protection, often used for estate planning and shielding wealth from lawsuits.

- **Drawbacks:** Requires giving up control of the assets and must be carefully structured to avoid legal challenges.

Charitable Trust

- **Definition:** A trust created to benefit a charitable organization or cause.

- **Revocable or Irrevocable:** Generally **irrevocable**.

- **Purpose:** Allows the grantor to donate assets to charity while enjoying certain tax benefits.

- **Charitable Remainder Trust (CRT):** Provides income to the grantor or other beneficiaries for a period of time, with the remainder going to charity.

- **Charitable Lead Trust (CLT):** Pays income to a charity for a set period of time, after which the remaining assets go to the grantor's heirs or other beneficiaries.

- **Benefits:** Provides tax deductions, supports charitable causes, and can reduce estate taxes.

- **Drawbacks:** Assets are no longer available to the grantor after transfer.

Special Needs Trust (Supplemental Needs Trust)

- **Definition:** A trust established to provide for a disabled or special needs beneficiary without disqualifying them from government benefits (like Medicaid or SSI).

- **Revocable or Irrevocable:** Typically **irrevocable**.

- **Purpose:** Ensures the beneficiary has financial support without losing eligibility for public assistance.

- **Trustee:** A trustee manages the assets on behalf of the disabled beneficiary.

- **Benefits:** Allows the beneficiary to receive assets without jeopardizing their government benefits.

- **Drawbacks:** Must be carefully managed to comply with government regulations.

Spendthrift Trust

- **Definition:** A trust designed to prevent the beneficiary from squandering the trust assets by restricting their access.

- **Revocable or Irrevocable:** Typically **irrevocable**.

- **Purpose:** Protects the assets from being recklessly spent by the beneficiary or claimed by creditors.

- **Trustee:** The trustee manages and controls disbursements to the beneficiary.

- **Benefits:** Protects assets from creditors, lawsuits, and poor financial decisions by the beneficiary.

- **Drawbacks:** Beneficiaries may have limited access to the trust funds.

Qualified Terminable Interest Property (QTIP) Trust

- **Definition:** A trust that provides income to a surviving spouse for life, with the remainder going to other beneficiaries (usually children from a previous marriage) after the spouse's death.

- **Revocable or Irrevocable:** Typically **irrevocable** after the grantor's death.

- **Purpose:** Allows the grantor to provide for a surviving spouse while controlling how the trust assets are distributed after the spouse's death.

- **Trustee:** The trustee pays income to the surviving spouse, with the remaining assets distributed to final beneficiaries.

- **Benefits:** Provides for a spouse while ensuring that assets go to designated beneficiaries after the spouse's death.

- **Drawbacks:** Complex tax planning may be required.

Grantor Retained Annuity Trust (GRAT)

- **Definition:** An irrevocable trust where the grantor transfers assets but retains the right to receive annuity payments for a set term.

- **Purpose:** Used to minimize estate taxes by transferring future appreciation of assets to beneficiaries.

- **Trustee:** The trustee manages the assets and pays the annuity to the grantor.

- **Benefits:** Can help reduce estate taxes while providing income to the grantor.

- **Drawbacks:** If the grantor dies during the trust term, the remaining assets may be included in the estate for tax purposes.

Dynasty Trust

- **Definition:** A trust designed to pass wealth from generation to generation without incurring estate or generation-skipping transfer taxes.

- **Revocable or Irrevocable:** Typically **irrevocable**.

- **Purpose:** Preserves wealth for future generations while avoiding estate taxes.

- **Trustee:** The trustee manages the assets according to the trust's terms, often for multiple generations.

- **Benefits:** Provides long-term wealth protection and minimizes estate taxes.

- **Drawbacks:** Complex to set up and manage, and not allowed in all states.

Totten Trust

- **Definition:** A form of trust created by depositing funds in a bank account in the name of the depositor "as trustee for" a beneficiary.

- **Revocable or Irrevocable: Revocable** during the grantor's lifetime.

- **Purpose:** Allows the funds to pass to the beneficiary without probate.

- **Trustee:** The grantor serves as the trustee during their lifetime.

- **Benefits:** Simple and inexpensive way to pass assets upon death.

- **Drawbacks:** Only applies to bank accounts and cannot handle more complex asset structures.

Business Trust

- **Definition:** A trust used to manage business assets, where trustees manage the business on behalf of beneficiaries (shareholders).

- **Ownership:** Beneficiaries own certificates of beneficial interest, similar to shareholders owning stock.

- **Legal Liability:** Liability is limited to the trust's assets, protecting beneficiaries from personal liability.

- **Management:** Trustees manage the business and make decisions for the trust.

- **Taxes:** Can be treated as a partnership, corporation, or trust for tax purposes, depending on the structure.

- **Purpose:** Often used for investment funds or real estate holdings.

Most Protection from Personal Liability

Corporations (C-Corp or S-Corp)

- **Liability Protection:** Both **C-Corporations** and **S-Corporations** offer the strongest level of personal liability protection. Shareholders' personal assets are protected from business debts and liabilities, meaning they are only liable for the amount they have invested in the corporation.

- **Management Liability:** Officers and directors can also be protected from personal liability for corporate decisions, although this can vary based on negligence or other factors.

- **Drawbacks:** Increased complexity in management, regulatory requirements, and potential for double taxation (for C-Corp) or additional restrictions (for S-Corp).

Limited Liability Company (LLC)

- **Liability Protection:** LLCs provide strong personal liability protection for owners (members). Members are generally not personally responsible for the LLC's debts and legal obligations. Their liability is limited to their investment in the business.

- **Management Liability:** If the LLC is properly structured and operated (following corporate formalities), even managers or managing members of the LLC are protected from personal liability.

- **Drawbacks:** Fewer formalities than a corporation, but members must still adhere to certain legal and financial separations (like not mixing personal and business assets).

Limited Liability Partnership (LLP)

- **Liability Protection:** In an **LLP**, each partner is shielded from liability for the actions or negligence of other partners.

Personal assets are protected from the partnership's debts and liabilities, except for individual malpractice or wrongful actions.

- **Management Liability:** Partners have personal liability protection but must remain cautious of personal actions and responsibilities in the business.

- **Drawbacks:** Primarily designed for professional firms (like law, medical, or accounting practices) and less suitable for non-professional businesses.

Asset Protection Trust

- **Liability Protection: Asset Protection Trusts** (particularly **Domestic Asset Protection Trusts** and **Offshore Asset Protection Trusts**) offer some of the strongest protections from creditors, lawsuits, and liability claims. Assets placed into these trusts are shielded from creditors, though they remain available for the beneficiaries.

- **Drawbacks:** Trusts are typically designed for estate planning or protecting personal assets and not for running a business.

Trademark

A **trademark** is a recognizable sign, symbol, word, phrase, logo, or combination of these that identifies and distinguishes the source of goods or services of one company from those of others. Trademarks are used to protect the brand and help consumers recognize and trust the products or services associated with the mark.

When a trademark is legally registered, the owner gains exclusive rights to use the mark in connection with specific goods or services, and it prevents others from using a confusingly similar mark in the same industry. Trademarks help protect a company's reputation and intellectual property by ensuring that no other business can unfairly benefit from their brand.

Trademarks can include:

- Words (e.g., "Ardass")

- Logos (e.g., Ardass Corporation)

- Phrases (e.g., "Name of Trust")

- Designs, symbols, or even colors or sounds that represent a brand.

A trademark is typically registered with a government agency, such as the **United States Patent and Trademark Office (USPTO)**, to secure legal protection.

Generic Trademark

- **Definition:** These are common words or terms used to describe a general product or service. They are **not eligible for trademark protection** because they are too generic.

- **Example:** "Bicycle" for a bicycle company.

- **Note:** Generic terms cannot be trademarked because they are commonly used by the public to refer to a class of products or services.

Descriptive Trademark

- **Definition:** These describe a specific quality, characteristic, or feature of a product or service. They are usually hard to protect unless they have acquired **secondary meaning** (when the public associates the term with a particular source).

- **Example:** "Cold and Creamy" for ice cream.

- **Note:** Descriptive trademarks can be registered if they become distinct over time through usage.

Suggestive Trademark

- **Definition:** Suggestive trademarks hint at a characteristic or quality of the product without explicitly describing it. They are inherently **protectable** without needing to prove secondary meaning.

- **Example:** "Netflix" suggests internet and movies.

- **Note:** These marks require the consumer to use some imagination to connect the name with the product or service.

Arbitrary Trademark

- **Definition:** Arbitrary trademarks use common words that have no relation to the product or service they represent. They are inherently **strong trademarks** and easy to protect.

- **Example:** "Apple" for computers.

- **Note:** These marks are highly protectable because they are unrelated to the actual product or service.

Fanciful Trademark

- **Definition:** These are made-up or invented words that have no prior meaning. They are the **strongest type of trademark** and are highly protectable.

- **Example:** "Xerox" for photocopiers, "Kodak" for cameras.

- **Note:** Fanciful trademarks are unique and distinctive from the start.

Service Mark

- **Definition:** A service mark is similar to a trademark but is used to identify and distinguish the services of one provider from others, rather than a product.

- **Example:** "FedEx" for delivery services.

- **Note:** Service marks are often used by businesses that provide services rather than physical goods.

Collective Mark

- **Definition:** A trademark used by members of a collective group or association to indicate membership or association with the group.

- **Example:** "CPA" used by Certified Public Accountants.

- **Note:** Collective marks are used to represent a group or organization's standards or membership.

Certification Mark

- **Definition:** A mark used to certify that a product or service meets specific standards set by the owner of the mark (such as material, quality, or origin).

- **Example:** "Fair Trade Certified" for ethically sourced goods.

- **Note:** Certification marks are not used by the owner but are licensed to others to show compliance with set standards.

Trade Dress

- **Definition:** A form of trademark that protects the overall look, design, packaging, or appearance of a product that signifies its source.

- **Example:** The shape of a Coca-Cola bottle or the design of an iPhone.

- **Note:** Trade dress must be distinctive and not functional to be eligible for protection.

*****

Copyright

Copyright is a legal protection granted to the creators of original works, such as literature, music, art, film, and more. It gives the creator exclusive rights to control how their work is used, reproduced, distributed, and displayed. Copyright protects the **expression of ideas** (the creative content) but not the ideas themselves.

When a work is copyrighted, the creator has the exclusive right to:

1. **Reproduce** the work (make copies).

2. **Distribute** copies to the public.

3. **Perform** or display the work publicly.

4. **Create derivative works**, such as adaptations or translations.

Copyright protection starts automatically when an original work is fixed in a tangible form, such as writing it down or recording it. The creator doesn't have to register their work, although registration with a government office (like the U.S. Copyright Office) can provide additional legal benefits. Copyright ensures that creators are rewarded for their intellectual effort and that others cannot use their work without permission.

Literary Work

- **Definition:** Protects written works such as books, articles, novels, poetry, essays, and even computer software code.

- **Examples:** Novels, poems, plays, academic papers, software code.

- **Protection:** Covers the expression of ideas in a tangible medium, but not the ideas themselves.

Musical Work

- **Definition:** Protects original musical compositions, including the music itself and any accompanying lyrics.

- **Examples:** Songs, symphonies, jingles.

- **Protection:** Covers both the musical score and the lyrics (if any).

Sound Recording

- **Definition:** Protects the actual recording of a musical or other type of audio performance.

- **Examples:** A recorded song, podcast episode, audiobook.

- **Protection:** Applies to the recorded performance, but not to the underlying musical composition or script.

Dramatic Works

- **Definition:** Protects works intended for performance, including scripts for theater, television, and film.

- **Examples:** Plays, screenplays, TV scripts.

- **Protection:** Covers the dialogue, staging, and other elements of a dramatic work.

Pantomimes and Choreographic Works

- **Definition:** Protects original works of choreography and dance routines, as well as non-verbal performance art (pantomimes).

- **Examples:** Ballets, dance routines, mime performances.

- **Protection:** Must be recorded or notated in a tangible form to be protected.

Pictorial, Graphic, and Sculptural Works

- **Definition:** Protects visual artworks, including photographs, paintings, drawings, sculptures, and more.

- **Examples:** Paintings, sculptures, photographs, illustrations, architectural drawings.

- **Protection:** Covers the visual expression of ideas but not the physical object itself.

Motion Pictures and Other Audiovisual Work

- **Definition:** Protects movies, television shows, video games, and other works that combine images and sound.

- **Examples:** Films, TV shows, video games, animated series.

- **Protection:** Applies to the visual and audio elements in a combined format.

Architectural Work

- **Definition:** Protects the design of buildings and other structures, both the original plans and the completed work.

- **Examples:** Blueprints, building designs, the structure of a completed building.

- **Protection:** Covers both the plans and the design of the completed structure, but not the functional elements like windows or doors.

Derivative Work

- **Definition:** Protects works based on or derived from existing works, such as translations, adaptations, or sequels.

- **Examples:** Movie adaptations of books, translations of novels, sequels to films.

- **Protection:** The original creator retains rights to their work, and the new creator has rights to the modifications or additions.

Compilations and Collective Work

- **Definition:** Protects collections of pre-existing works, such as anthologies, databases, or magazines.

- **Examples:** Anthologies of short stories, database compilations, encyclopedias.

- **Protection:** Applies to the selection, coordination, or arrangement of the works, not the individual works themselves.

*****

Patent

A **patent** is a government-granted legal right that gives an inventor exclusive control over making, using, selling, or distributing their invention for a limited time. In return, the inventor must publicly disclose details about the invention. Patents protect inventions or discoveries that are new, useful, and non-obvious. This legal protection prevents others from using or commercializing the invention without the inventor's permission, ensuring that the inventor benefits from their innovation while encouraging public access to new knowledge. Patents typically last for 20 years, depending on the type of invention.

Utility Patent

- **Definition:** This is the most common type of patent, granted for new, useful, and non-obvious inventions or discoveries related to processes, machines, manufactured products, or compositions of matter.

- **Examples:** A new kind of smartphone technology, A new chemical compound or drug, An innovative manufacturing process.

- **Duration:** Utility patents are generally valid for **20 years** from the filing date.

- **Purpose:** Protects the functional aspects of an invention, ensuring that no one else can make, use, or sell the invention without permission.

Design Patent

- **Definition:** Granted for new, original, and ornamental designs applied to an article of manufacture. It protects the appearance or aesthetic design rather than the functional features.

- **Examples:** The unique shape or surface ornamentation of a car, The distinctive look of a piece of furniture, A specific design for a beverage bottle.

- **Duration:** Design patents last for **15 years** from the grant date (in the U.S.).

- **Purpose:** Protects the visual, non-functional aspects of a product.

Plant Patent

- **Definition:** Granted to anyone who invents or discovers and asexually reproduces a new and distinct variety of plant. This includes plants that can be reproduced through means other than seeds, such as grafting or cuttings.

- **Examples:** A new variety of fruit trees, A new strain of flowering plants.

- **Duration:** Plant patents are valid for **20 years** from the filing date.

- **Purpose:** Protects the rights to reproduce, use, or sell the new plant variety.

Provisional Patent

A **temporary patent** that gives inventors a 12-month period to file for a full utility patent. It allows inventors to claim "patent pending" status while they continue to refine their inventions.

Non-Provisional Patent

A **regular utility patent application**, which starts the formal examination process to determine if the invention qualifies for a full utility patent.

*****

Constitution

A **constitution** is a set of fundamental principles, rules, and guidelines that outline how an organization, government, or entity is structured and operates. It serves as the highest form of law or regulation within the entity and defines its members' roles, rights, and duties. It also provides the framework for decision-making and governance.

Key Elements

1. **Preamble**: A statement of purpose that explains the reasons for the constitution and the goals of the entity it governs.

2. **Articles or Sections**: The main body of the constitution, which outlines the structure of the organization, the powers of different governing bodies, the rights and responsibilities of its members, and procedures for amending the constitution.

3. **Rights and Responsibilities**: Defines the rights of individuals or members, such as freedom of speech or voting rights, and their responsibilities within the entity.

4. **Governance Structure**: Details the structure of the governing bodies, such as the executive, legislative, and judicial branches (in a government) or the board of directors and officers (in a company or organization).

5. **Amendment Procedures**: Explains how changes or amendments to the constitution can be made over time.

Types

- **National Constitution**: A legal document that governs a country or nation, outlining its system of government and the rights of its citizens (e.g., the U.S. Constitution).

- **Corporate Constitution**: Also known as **bylaws**, a corporate constitution governs the internal functioning of a company or organization, including its management and operational guidelines.

- **Organizational Constitution**: Used by associations, clubs, or non-profit organizations to set out their purpose, governance, and procedures.

*****

By-Laws

Bylaws are formal rules and guidelines a corporation, organization, or association establishes that govern its operations. They outline the internal structure and procedures, such as the roles and responsibilities of board members, how meetings are conducted, how decisions are made, and how disputes are handled. They serve as the organization's internal governing document, ensuring consistency in its operations and decision-making processes.

Key Elements

1. **Board of Directors**: Defines how the board is structured, how members are appointed, and their duties and responsibilities.

2. **Meetings**: Outlines the frequency, procedures, and requirements for board or member meetings.

3. **Officer Roles:** Describes officers' roles, such as the president, treasurer, and secretary.

4. **Voting Procedures**: Specifies how votes are cast and counted, and what constitutes a quorum for making decisions.

5. **Amendments:** Explains how the bylaws can be changed or amended over time.

Purpose

- **Operational Consistency:** Ensures the organization follows a clear and organized process.

- **Legal Compliance:** Helps ensure the organization complies with legal requirements.

- **Decision-Making:** Provides a decision-making framework, minimizing confusion or disputes.

*****

Operating Agreement

An **Operating Agreement** is a legal document that outlines the ownership, management structure, and operational guidelines of a **Limited Liability Company (LLC)**. It serves as an internal document among the LLC members (owners), defining their roles, responsibilities, and the rules governing the business.

Key Elements

1. **Ownership Structure**: Specifies each member's ownership percentage in the LLC.

2. **Management Structure**: Defines whether the LLC will be **member-managed** (run by the owners) or **manager-managed** (where one or more managers run the business).

3. **Profit and Loss Distribution:** Details how profits and losses will be divided among members.

4. **Voting Rights:** Describes how decisions will be made, including the voting process and the weight of each member's vote.

5. **Membership Changes**: Explains how new members can join or how existing members can leave the LLC.

6. **Dissolution Procedures**: Outlines what happens if the LLC is dissolved, including how assets are distributed.

Purpose

- **Clarifies Expectations**: Establishes clear guidelines for the members' rights and responsibilities.

- **Prevents Disputes**: Minimizes conflicts by setting decision-making and resolution rules.

- **Customizes LLC Structure**: Allows LLC members to customize how the business operates beyond the default state laws.

- **Legal Protection**: Strengthens the limited liability protection of the members by demonstrating the LLC operates as a separate legal entity.

*****

Minutes

Minutes refer to the official written record of the discussions, decisions, and actions during a formal meeting. Minutes are typically used in business, legal, and organizational settings to document what transpired during board meetings, shareholder meetings, or committee meetings.

Key Elements

1. **Date and Time**: The meeting's time, date, and location.

2. **Attendance**: A list of who was present, including board members, officers, or other participants.

3. **Agenda Items**: A summary of the topics discussed during the meeting.

4. **Decisions Made**: Any formal decisions, resolutions, or votes taken, along with the outcome of those votes.

5. **Action Items**: Specific tasks or actions assigned to individuals or teams, along with deadlines.

6. **Approval of Previous Minutes**: In many organizations, the minutes from the previous meeting are reviewed and approved at the beginning of the current meeting.

Purpose

- **Official Record**: Provides an official record of decisions and discussions.

- **Legal Compliance**: Some organizations are legally required to maintain minutes to comply with governance or regulatory requirements.

- **Reference**: Acts as a reference for participants to review what was discussed or agreed upon in previous meetings.

- **Accountability**: Tracks action items and responsibilities assigned during the meeting.

*****

Director

A **director** is a part of a company or organization's board of directors and oversees its overall management and decision-making. Directors are typically elected by shareholders and are tasked with guiding the company's strategic direction, making important business decisions, and ensuring the company operates in the best interests of its stakeholders.

Key Responsibilities

1. **Strategic Oversight**: Directors help shape the company's long-term strategy, setting goals and ensuring the company follows its mission.

2. **Fiduciary Duty**: Directors have a fiduciary duty to act in the company's and its shareholders' best interests, making responsible financial and managerial decisions.

3. **Hiring Executives**: Directors may hire and oversee key executives, such as the CEO, and ensure they effectively manage the company's day-to-day operations.

4. **Compliance**: Directors ensure the company complies with laws and regulations and upholds ethical standards.

5. **Approving Major Decisions**: Directors approve significant corporate actions, such

as mergers, acquisitions, issuing stock, and financial matters.

Types

- **Executive Director**: A director with a management role in the company, such as the CEO or CFO.

- **Non-Executive Director**: A director who does not have an active role in daily management but provides oversight and guidance.

- **Independent Director**: A director not affiliated with the company in any other capacity, often included to provide unbiased oversight.

*****

Officer

An **officer** is an individual appointed by a company's board of directors to manage the day-to-day operations and execute the strategic plans of the business. Officers hold positions of authority within the company and oversee specific areas, such as finance, operations, or legal compliance. Common officer titles include **Chief Executive Officer (CEO)**, **Chief Financial Officer (CFO)**, **Chief Operating Officer (COO)**, and **Secretary**.

Key Responsibilities

1. **Day-to-day Management**: Officers are responsible for the company's daily operations and ensure that business activities align with the company's goals and policies.

2. **Implementing Strategy**: Officers take the strategic decisions made by the board of directors and turn them into actionable plans and objectives.

3. **Reporting to the Board**: Officers regularly report to the board of directors, providing updates on business performance and key activities.

4. **Supervising Employees:** Officers oversee different departments or functions, providing leadership to employees and ensuring smooth business operations.

5. **Legal Compliance** – Officers ensure the company complies with legal and regulatory requirements.

Types

- **CEO (Chief Executive Officer)**: The highest-ranking officer in the company, responsible for the overall management and leadership.

- **CFO (Chief Financial Officer)**: Manages the company's finances, including budgeting, financial reporting, and investments.

- **COO (Chief Operating Officer)**: Oversees daily operations, ensuring the company runs efficiently.

- **Secretary**: Responsible for maintaining company records, ensuring regulatory compliance, and managing corporate governance matters.

*****

Key Employee

A **key employee** is an individual within an organization who holds a critical role and makes significant contributions to the success of the business. These employees typically have specialized skills, experience, or decision-making authority that directly impacts the company's operations, growth, or profitability. They may also hold leadership positions or have unique knowledge that is vital to the business's competitive edge.

Key employees are often irreplaceable in the short term and may include executives, senior managers, or highly skilled professionals. Due to their importance, companies may offer key employees special compensation packages or benefits to retain them.

*****

Employee

An **employee** is a person who works for a company or organization under an employment contract or agreement, where they provide labor or services in exchange for a salary or wages. Employees are typically under the direction and control of the employer regarding how, when, and where they work.

Employees often receive benefits such as health insurance, retirement plans, and paid leave, and they are subject to taxes and legal protections under labor laws, such as minimum wage, overtime pay, and workplace safety standards. The employer withholds income taxes, Social Security, and Medicare contributions on behalf of the employee.

*****

Employee-Employer Relationship

The **employee-employer relationship** refers to the legal and working arrangement between an individual (employee) and the company or organization (employer) they work for. In this relationship, the employee agrees to perform specific tasks or duties under the employer's direction and control in exchange for compensation, such as a salary or wages.

The employer provides the employee with resources, tools, and guidance necessary to complete their job and is responsible for providing benefits, withholding taxes, and adhering to labor laws. In return, the employee is expected to follow the employer's policies, fulfill their job responsibilities, and contribute to the organization's success.

*****

Independent Contractor

An **independent contractor** is a self-employed individual or business hired to perform specific tasks or services for another company or individual. They are not considered employees. Independent contractors control how they complete their work, typically use their own tools and equipment, and are paid per project or assignment rather than receiving a salary or hourly wage.

Unlike employees, independent contractors are responsible for their own taxes, including self-employment taxes, and they do not receive benefits like health insurance or retirement plans from the company they work for. Common examples include freelancers, consultants, and contractors in various industries.

*****

Acknowledgment

I want to express my deepest gratitude to my beloved wife, Rupinder Kaur, whose unwavering support was the bedrock of this journey. Her constant encouragement, love, and motivation have been my source of strength through every challenge, both in

Rupinder Kaur

business and life. She has stood by me with patience and understanding, offering wisdom and resilience that have guided me during the ups and downs. Without her belief in me, this book would not have been possible. Rupinder Kaur's steadfast presence has allowed me to focus on my goals and confidently pursue my vision. She has been not only my partner in life but also the driving force behind every success. This accomplishment is as much hers as it is mine. Thank you, Rupinder Kaur, for your endless support and belief in me.

*****

www.ingramcontent.com/pod-product-compliance
Lightning Source LLC
Chambersburg PA
CBHW031225120626
46545CB00003B/988